★ RODEO ★

RODEO

The Great American Sport

by MURRAY TINKELMAN

★ Greenwillow Books, New York ★

ACKNOWLEDGMENTS

A very special thanks to Dan Civitello for his early support and encouragement and for introducing me to the Crotta family, Paul, Paulie, Wyatt, Mark, Janice, Kim, and Mexico, who shared their time, skills, and knowledge so warmly and through whom I met Grant and Betsy Harris of Cowtown, New Jersey, whose patience and hospitality contributed so greatly to the making of this book. Thanks also to Tony Bartolini, Pat and Brian DuBois, Steve Foster, Ginger Hallaman, Charlie Parks, and all the cowboys and cowgirls whose images appear in this book.

A most important thanks to Ken Stemler, Dave Baldridge, and Kristine Fredriksson of The Professional Rodeo Cowboys Association, without whom this book would not have been possible.

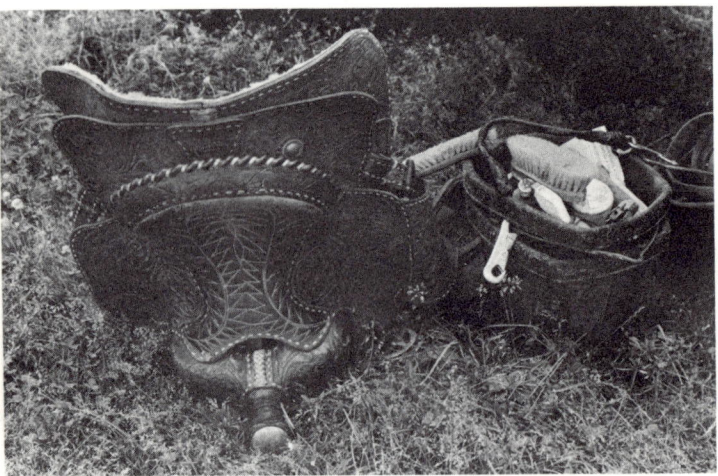

Copyright © 1982 by Murray Tinkelman
All rights reserved. No part of this book may be reproduced or utilized in any form or by any means, electronic or mechanical, including photocopying, recording or by any information storage and retrieval system, without permission in writing from the Publisher, Greenwillow Books, a division of William Morrow & Company, Inc., 105 Madison Avenue, New York, N.Y. 10016.

Printed in the United States of America
First Edition

10 9 8 7 6 5 4 3 2

Art direction and design
by Ava Weiss with Mina Greenstein

Library of Congress
Cataloging in Publication Data

Tinkelman, Murray.
Rodeo.

Summary: Bronc riding, calf roping, bull dogging, bull riding, and other rodeo events are described in the framework of a rodeo day.
1. Rodeos—Juvenile literature.
[1. Rodeos] I. Title.
GV1834.T54   791'.8   81-6359
ISBN 0-688-00841-0 (lib. bdg.)   AACR2
ISBN 0-688-01194-2 (pbk.)

For Carol
who hauls good

There was never a hoss that couldn't be rode
and never a rider that couldn't be throwed.
—Old Saying

EVENTS

Introduction, 11

Bareback Riding, 24

Calf Roping, 28

Saddle-Bronc Riding, 34

Steer Wrestling, 40

Barrel Racing, 44

Team Roping, 48

Bull Riding, 52

INTRODUCTION

Rodeo, Spanish for "roundup," is unique. It is the only professional sport that has its origins in an actual workaday occupation, cattle ranching. The three classic events of modern rodeo, saddle-bronc riding, calf roping, and team roping, remain virtually unchanged from their frontier origins.

In the mid-1800s, the era of the great cattle drives, the working cowboy had to be an able hand at roping livestock and riding half-tamed horses. Before the annual autumn drive could begin, roundups were held to separate one rancher's cattle from another's. Calves had to be caught and branded, dangerous 600-pound longhorn steers had to be roped by a team of two cowboys when the steers needed doctoring, and wild horses had to be broken to the saddle. It was grueling, backbreaking, dawn-to-dusk work that allowed little rest and exposed the cowboys to constant physical danger.

Yet, after their work was done, it became common practice for the top hands of one ranch to match their skills against the best cowboys of a neighboring ranch. These contests, to ride the unridable horse and to out-rope fellow cowpokes, spread in popularity and are the roots of modern rodeo.

Many towns in the southwest claim the honor of staging the first rodeo. It's said that the first rodeo to offer prize money to contestants was in Pecos, Texas, in 1883, and the Prescott, Arizona, rodeo of 1888 is supposed to be the first one that charged admission to the public. The specific origins of rodeo, however, are

lost in history. What we may assume is that somewhere some cowboy said, "I can ride that horse, and I got some money here to prove it." Dusty corrals and trail camps were the scene of those early battles between man and animal, and although the settings are different today, the contest is the same.

When the rodeo announcer says, "Let's rodeo!" what you are about to see is a spectacular and popular sport performed by highly skilled athletes.

Unlike most professional athletes, the rodeo cowboys and cowgirls are not members of teams, they have no clubhouse, trainers, team doctors, organized cheerleaders, team planes or buses. They pay all their own expenses to and from the rodeo, and must pay an entry fee for every event in which they participate. If they do not win or place in the prize money, their only reward is the memory of the crowd's applause. However, there are winners, big winners. The National Finals Rodeo, which is held annually, is now a five hundred thousand dollar event that is rodeo's counterpart to the world series or super bowl. In addition to prize money, engraved belt buckles are awarded for each event.

Spectacular as they are, it takes more than daredevil riders and ropers to make a rodeo. From planning committees and publicists to hot dog salesmen, endless hours are spent in organizing and presenting a successful show.

Bucking horses, bulls, steers, calves, where do they come from? The stock contractors have the responsibility for supplying the rodeo with sound and willing livestock. The contractors have an enormous investment in these animals, as well as in the vehicles used to transport them. A good bucking horse may

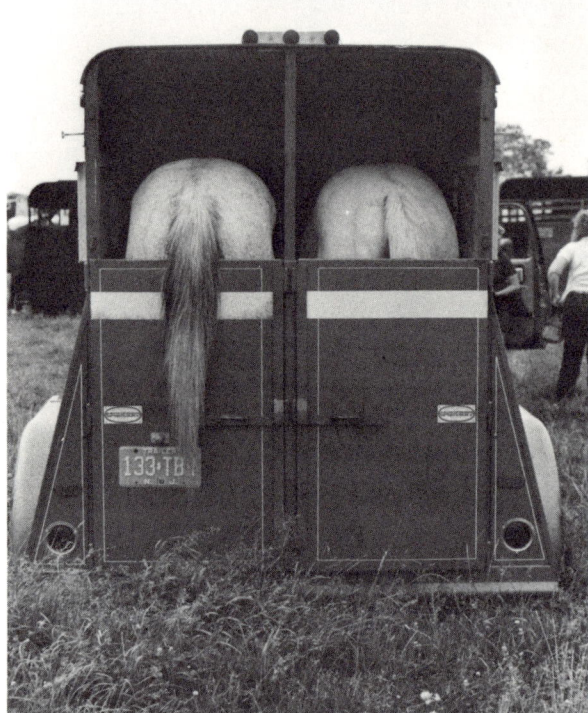

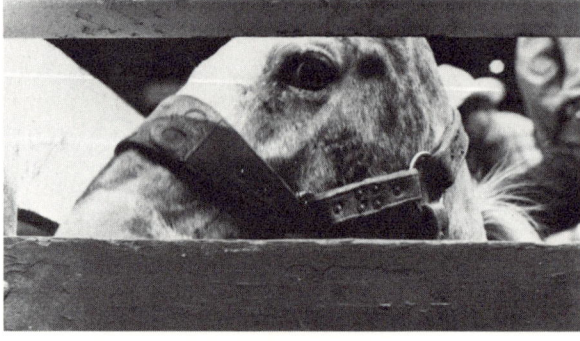

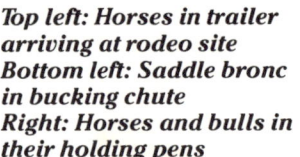

Top left: Horses in trailer arriving at rodeo site
Bottom left: Saddle bronc in bucking chute
Right: Horses and bulls in their holding pens

Behind the chutes, bronc and bull riders put on their boots and buckle on their spurs

cost as much as five thousand dollars and a "rank" or mean bull might be worth thirty-five hundred dollars. These animals receive the best of care and may "work" the grand total of ten to twelve minutes a year. There are champion bucking horses that are twenty-five to thirty years of age, often older than the cowboys who attempt to ride them.

Who rides what? The term "luck of the draw" accurately describes how the cowboys are matched with their four-footed adversaries. All livestock used in rodeo events are drawn by number from a hat by a rodeo judge or, more recently, by computer, and posted in advance of the rodeo.

Whether it's pronounced "ro-day-o" as it is in the southwest, or "ro-dee-o" in the north and east, the action is presented by the rodeo announcer. For two or three hours, he maintains a steady stream of patter. He must identify the contestants, describe the events, and fill the time between the events with colorful commentary. Many spectators will remember the announcer best as the "straight man" for the rodeo clowns. He will patiently repeat the clown's banter over the microphone for the audience to hear and will inevitably be the butt of the oldest, corniest, and most outrageously funny punch lines heard since vaudeville.

Rodeo cowboys and cowgirls come from widely diverse backgrounds. Some, of course, come from ranches or farms. Others come from college rodeo teams or high school teams, and youngsters may start in little britches rodeo. There are rodeo schools and clinics throughout the country where future rodeo performers can sharpen their skills. There is one characteristic, however, that binds these individuals together. Although competing directly against one another for prize money, they are totally supportive of each other. A bronc or bull rider will applaud a rival's good performance. Information about the bucking characteristics or tricks of a particular horse or bull is given freely by riders who know the animals. The ropers will also share their information on how a steer or calf acts when leaving the roping chute. These gestures are not isolated occurrences, they symbolize the spirit of rodeo. ★

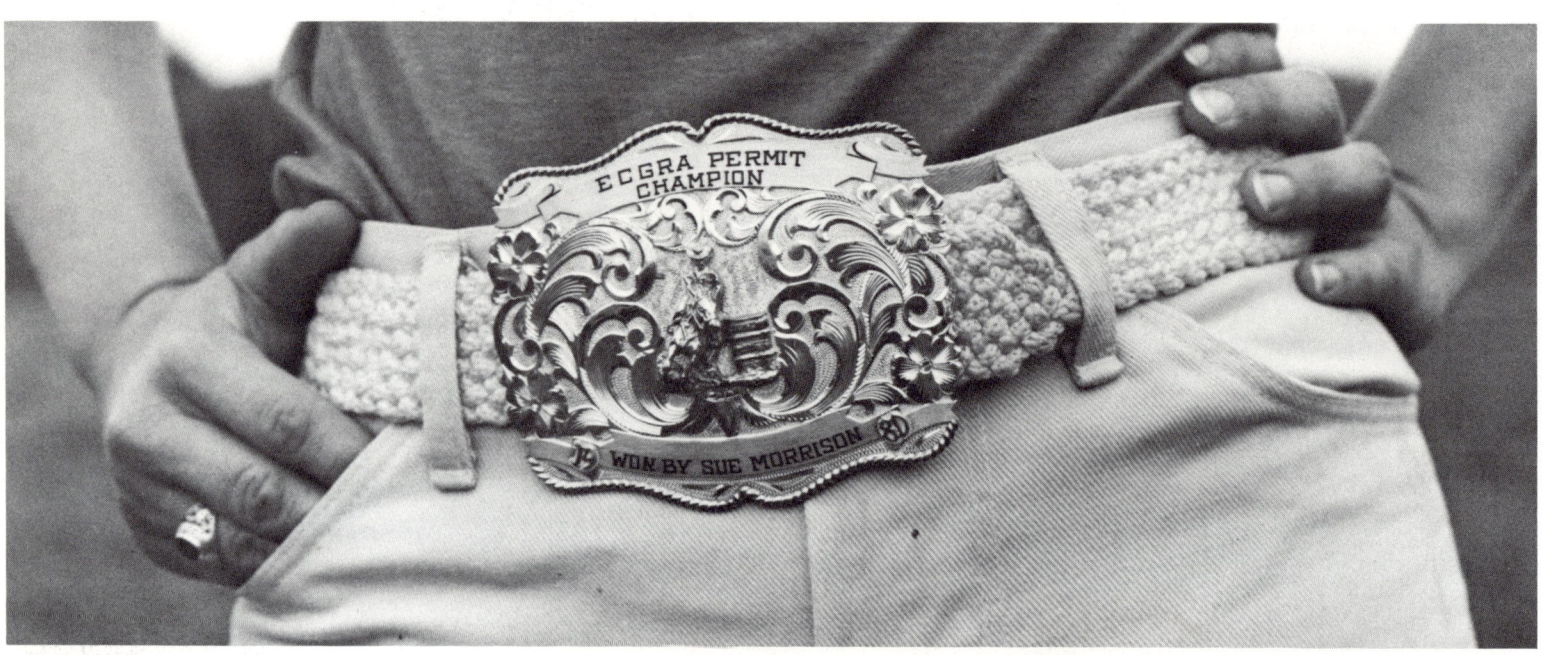

"Buckles will be awarded for every event!"
The buckles are often elaborately engraved.
Some are embellished with precious metals and gems

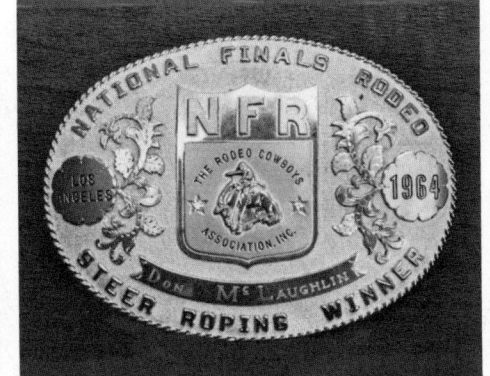

Left to right: Bull rider examines his rope Bullfighting clown adjusts his protective knee braces A farrier makes a last-minute replacement of a faulty shoe

Behind the scenes. A bull rider examines his bull rope. A young bareback rider waits patiently for his event

Top: Saddle-bronc rider adjusts the stirrups of his saddle. These standardized saddles are known as association saddles
Bottom: Saddle-bronc rider "stretches out" his saddle

Rodeo's informal setting encourages close contact between spectators and performers

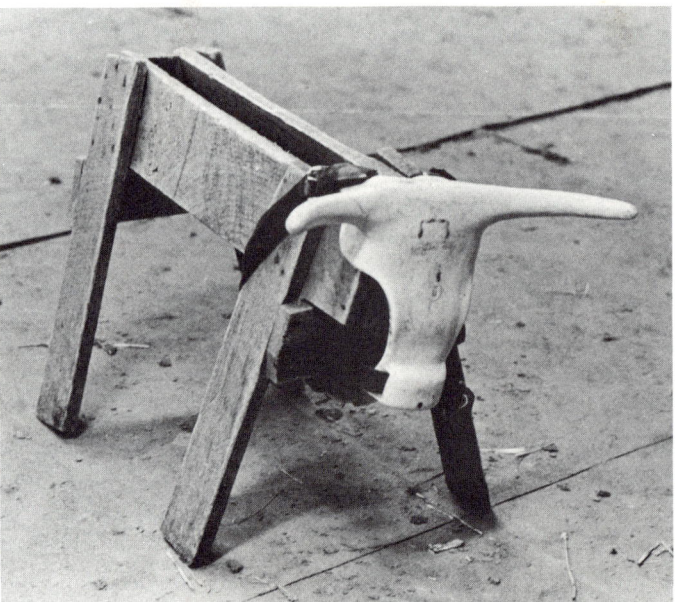
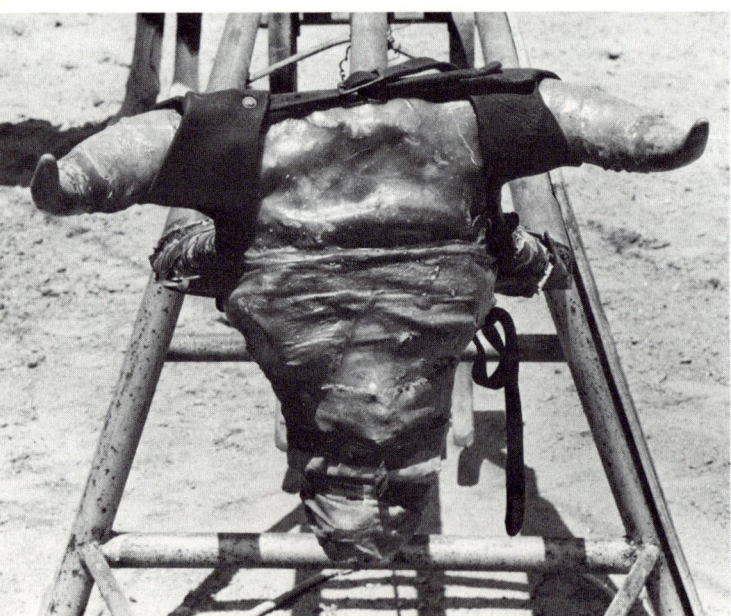

Roping dummies are used by the ropers for warm-up practice before their events. They differ in appearance from rodeo to rodeo. These dummies are handmade, highly individual facsimiles of steers. Some are stationary, others are designed to be dragged behind a horse for ropers to practice with a moving target. They may be considered as a unique form of American folk art

Team-roping "header" practicing his toss on a finely crafted wooden steer

Bird's-eye view of the bucking chutes in the foreground and the holding pens in the rear

20

Pender County Library
Hampstead Branch

Rodeo cowboys and cowgirls performing the serpentine grand entry march, the traditional opening ceremony of the rodeo. The brightly colored banners represent the fifty states of the Union

"Miss Rodeo" has the honor of displaying the Stars and Stripes during the playing of the national anthem

BAREBACK RIDING

"Bareback riders, get ready, your horses are in the chutes," calls the announcer. As in the other "rough stock" events—saddle-bronc and bull riding—the bareback rider mounts from the top of the bucking chute. He rides without a saddle, reins, or stirrups. The handhold, that he grips with his gloved hand, looks like a suitcase handle and is the top part of a leather rigging. The rigging is placed around the horse just behind the shoulders. In all rough stock events, a flank strap encircles the animal behind the curve of its belly. This flank does not cause the animal any pain, but it is a foreign object and makes the horse buck harder to try to get rid of it. To make a qualified ride, the cowboy must have his spurs over the break of the horse's shoulders when the bronc's front feet touch the ground on the first jump out of the chute and he must continue spurring throughout the eight-second ride. This is called "marking the horse out." The cowboy must not touch himself, the equipment, or the horse with his free hand, or he will be disqualified. ★

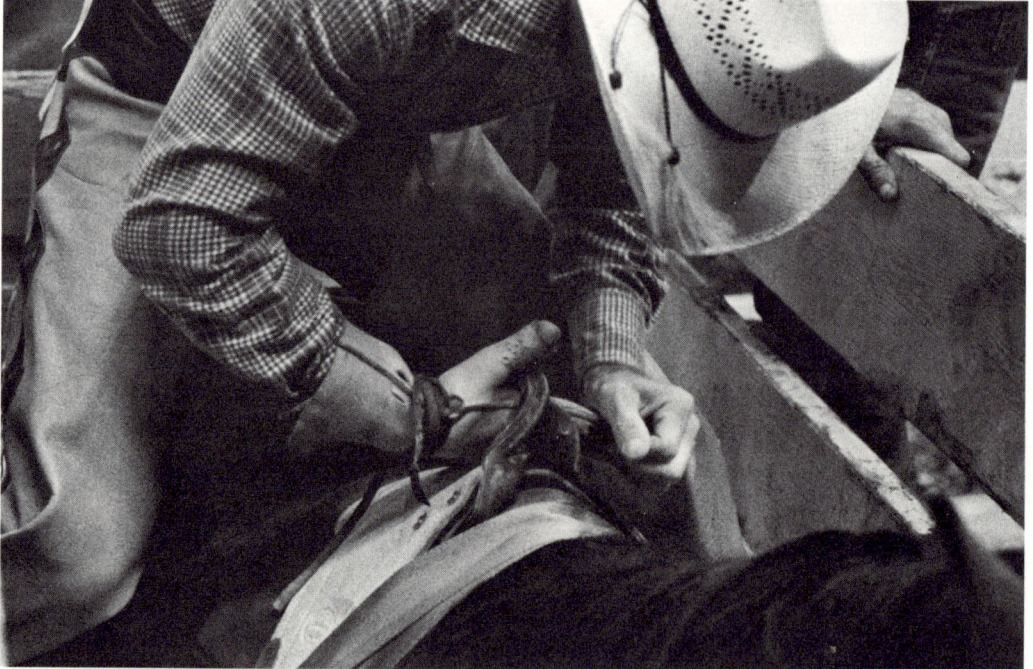

Top: Bareback rider about to mount his bronc

Bottom: Bareback rider fits his heavily rosined glove into the handle part of the rigging. The rosin allows the rider to maintain a firmer grip during his ride

Hat flying, chaps flaring, the bareback rider has his spurs well over the break of the horse's shoulders in classic style

Bareback riders and broncs in action

*"Crash city!" A flying spill.
Pick-up man stands by*

CALF ROPING

Calf roping is one of the oldest events in rodeo. It originated on the ranches and open ranges of the old west. During the spring roundups, calves were roped from horseback for branding or doctoring. In modern rodeo, the calves are permitted to break the barrier string first as they leave the chute and so get a head start. If the cowboy breaks the barrier by leaving the roping box too soon, he has a ten-second penalty added to his time. The cowboy may carry an extra loop or lariat in case he misses his first throw. The roper must make his "catch" from horseback, then dismount, run down the rope which is being held taut by his highly trained horse, throw the two hundred to three hundred pound calf to the ground, and cross and tie any three of the calf's legs with the six-foot "piggen" string that he carries in his teeth. If the calf stumbles or falls to the ground before the roper reaches it, he must let it rise and throw it by hand. He then throws his hands high in the air to signal the finish. The "tie," which is a half hitch or "hooey," must hold for six seconds after the roper remounts his horse and slacks the rope. ★

The calf roper makes a quick catch as the calf breaks from the roping chute

Calf roper, a study in concentration, as he prepares himself in the roping box

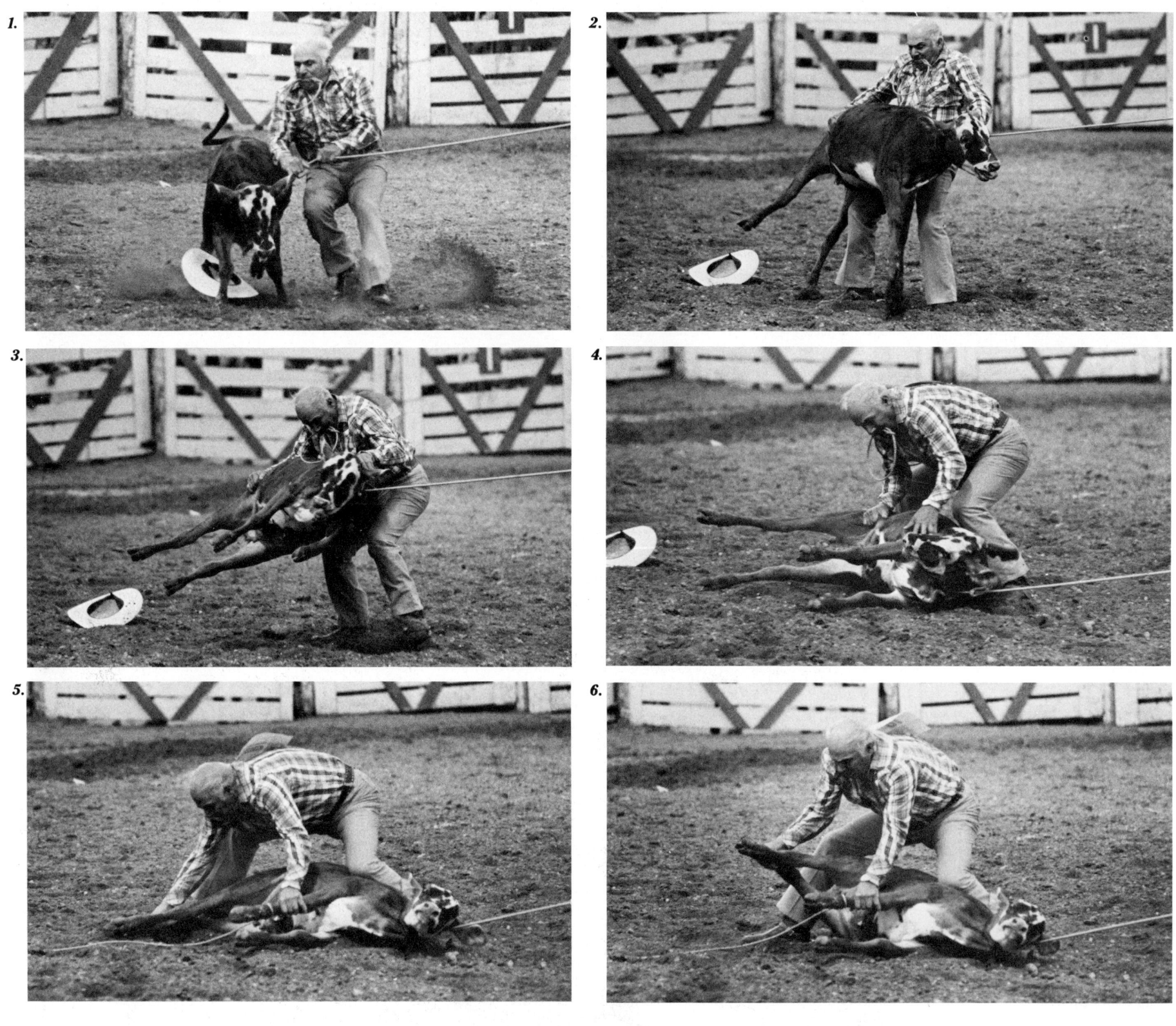

Opposite: Sequence showing calf roper "flanking" or throwing the calf to the ground so that he can make the required tie

The calf roper's signal to the timers that he has completed his event and the clock can be stopped

The calf roper has made his catch and is dismounting as his horse starts backing to remove the slack from the rope

*Bottom left: Fellow cowboys look on as calf roper and calf hit the dirt together
Right: A calf roper misses his toss*

Two judges may award up to fifty points to the horse and fifty points to the rider for the one hundred points available for each ride. It is interesting to note that the mount is also considered an athlete and is scored accordingly. Occasionally the bronc or cowboy does not have a fair opportunity to show his best. For example, a horse may get so excited in the chute that it can't be mounted, or a rider may be raked off on the chute gate. In such cases the judges award the cowboy a re-ride.

The two judges in this event are themselves experienced rodeo performers. With lightning speed each must determine whether the cowboy has made a qualified ride, and if he has, award the points allotted separately to rider and to mount. Both judges' points are then totaled for the final score. ★

Judge keeping score

SADDLE-BRONC RIDING

Top: Young saddle-bronc rider
Bottom: Fleece-lined flank strap

Saddle-bronc riding is rodeo's oldest event. It evolved from the need of early cowboys to "break" or tame wild horses for ranch and range work. Saddle-bronc riding may not be as flamboyant as the bareback event, but its requirements are subtler. The saddle-bronc rider does not depend on strength alone. Staying in the saddle requires timing, balance, and the ability to find the rhythm of the bucking horse. The rider has only the "buck rein," attached to the horse's halter, to hold onto, while his free hand is used for balance. As in the bareback event, the rider must have his spurs over the break of the horse's shoulders when the bronc's front feet touch the ground on the first jump out of the chute, and continue his spurring motion backward and forward throughout the eight-second ride. The buck rein and riding hand must be on the same side of the horse's head and neck. A rider is disqualified if he changes hands, loses a stirrup, touches himself or the horse with his free hand, or of course, is bucked off. A constant danger the saddle-bronc rider faces is having his boot caught in the stirrup when he is bucked off and being dragged by the bucking horse. Many saddle-bronc riders prefer boots that are slightly too large so they will pull off if the rider gets "hung up." As in bareback-bronc riding and bull riding, the two judges may award up to fifty points each to the horse and fifty points to the rider for the one hundred point possible score. ★

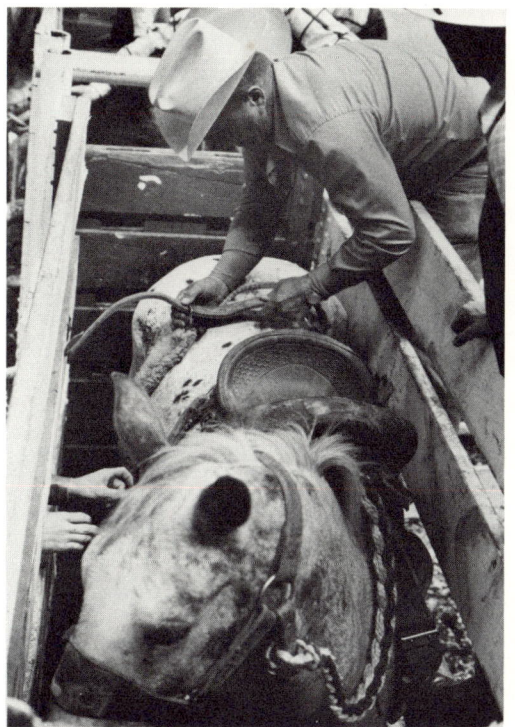
Cowboy adjusting flank strap

Saddle-bronc rider preparing to mount

Saddle-bronc riders in top form

Saddle-bronc rider spurring his mount during ride

A slow shutter speed shot of saddle-bronc event

Top: Saddle-bronc riders display their skill
Bottom: Bronc 1, Cowboy 0

A perfect ride in a muddy arena

38

The unsung heroes of the bronc riding events are the two pickup men. At the end of the hectic eight-second event, the pickup men ride in to assist the cowboy in getting off the still bucking and lunging horse. They then release the flank strap and chase the bronc back to the pens. ★

Pick-up man helps bareback rider off his bronc

Pick-up man and saddle-bronc rider

STEER WRESTLING

Bulldogging was introduced to rodeo in 1907 by Bill Pickett, a black cowboy nicknamed "The Dusky Demon." "Dogging," or "steer wrestling" as it is now called, went on to become a regular and popular rodeo event. The steer wrestler has a partner called a "hazer" to assist him during his run. When the 450 to 750 pound steer bursts from the chute, it trips a barrier line which sends the steer wrestler and hazer in hot pursuit. The hazer keeps the steer running in a straight line as the steer wrestler leaps off his speeding horse to get a solid grip on the steer's head and horns. This "catch" is made at about thirty-five miles per hour. The steer wrestler must then stop the steer and wrestle it to the ground. The steer is considered down only when it is lying flat with its head and all four feet pointing in the same direction. If the steer gets loose, the steer wrestler may take only one step to catch him. As in all timed events, the cowboy is assessed a ten-second penalty if he breaks the barrier line. A top steer wrestler may dog his steer in five seconds or less. ★

Steer wrestler ready to make his leap

Steer wrestler with firm grip on steer's head and horns, and one foot still in running horse's stirrup

"Down goes the price of beef." Strength, agility, and timing are needed to wrestle a steer to the ground

BARREL RACING

Barrel racing is the cowgirl's event. The racer may take a running start into the arena as she begins riding a cloverleaf pattern around three brightly colored barrels. The rider races for the first barrel, reins her horse sharply around it and makes for the second barrel, another tight turn and she heads for the last barrel at the far end of the arena. After the final barrel turn is made, she spurs her horse for the full-speed race back to the finish line. This timed event is relatively new in rodeo and is an exciting contrast to the rough stock and roping competitions. Electronic timers record the barrel racer's time from start to finish. A five-second penalty is added for any barrel tipped over during an event. Under seventeen seconds is considered excellent time for a completed course. ★

Barrel racers

Sequence showing last leg of the cloverleaf course

The last turn – rider and horse race for the finish line to the sound of the crowd's applause

The header prepares for his toss. The heeler follows with his lariat ready

TEAM ROPING

Team roping is the next event. It is performed the same way in the rodeo arena as it is on working ranches. The team consists of a "header" and a "heeler." As in calf roping, the steer is given a head start from the chute and the header must avoid breaking the barrier as he leaves the roping box. The header then ropes the seven hundred pound steer by the head, neck, or horns, takes a "dally" or two turns of his rope around the saddle horn, and turns the steer into position for the heeler to make his throw. The heeler lassos both of the steer's hind legs and dallies his rope. The header then turns his horse

Left: Team roper's saddle with strips of rubber wrapped around the dally horn to prevent the rope from slipping

Opposite: The header has made his catch. The heeler swings her lariat, about to make her heel toss

to face both the steer and the heeler and the judges' flag signals the time. A ten-second penalty is added to the time for breaking the barrier and a five-second penalty is added if the heeler catches only one hind leg. A clean catch of both hind legs is called a "double hocker." Good timing for this event is in the six-second range.

Team ropers will tell you that it is a good idea to keep your fingers clear of the dally. A lunging steer snapping the rope suddenly taut can trap a finger between the saddle horn and the rope, causing a painful and serious injury. ★

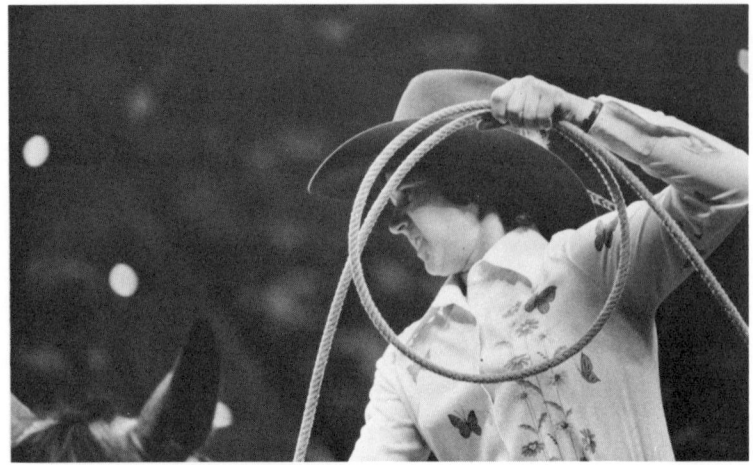
Team roper coiling her lariat

The header has turned the steer so the heeler can make his catch

The header's rope is dallied around the saddle horn. The heeler moves in close for his throw

Bull rider applies rosin to his bull rope. Rigging, chaps, and assorted gear hang on a side gate

BULL RIDING

Bull riding is usually the last event. It is the most dangerous. The bulls are heavier, up to two thousand pounds, and far less predictable than the bucking horses. They are amazingly agile for their size and are bred for their meanness. The bull rider slips his heavily gloved hand into the braided handhold of the flat plaited bull rope. The rope is then pulled tight around the bull and wrapped around the bull rider's hand. The rope has a bell attached which annoys it and makes the bull buck harder. The bulls that spin tightly while bucking are considered the most dangerous to ride. The bull rider is not allowed to touch himself, the bull, or the equipment with his free hand. Bull riding has been described by a rodeo announcer as "the sun, and all of the other events are like the planets revolving around it." It is a fitting finale to a day at the rodeo.

The rider often lies dazed and helpless on the ground when he has been thrown. The bull will not hesitate to go after him, hooking with its horns, butting and trampling. It is the job of the rodeo clown to distract the bull's attention and allow the cowboy to get to safety, which often means over the fence and out of the arena.

Another constant peril the bull rider faces is being "hung up." If he cannot free his tightly wrapped hand from the bull rope when he is thrown or the ride is ended, he is in danger of being flung helplessly about, like a rag doll, while the bull continues to buck and spin. Again it is the bullfighting clown who fearlessly rushes to the aid of the cowboy to free his trapped hand. ★

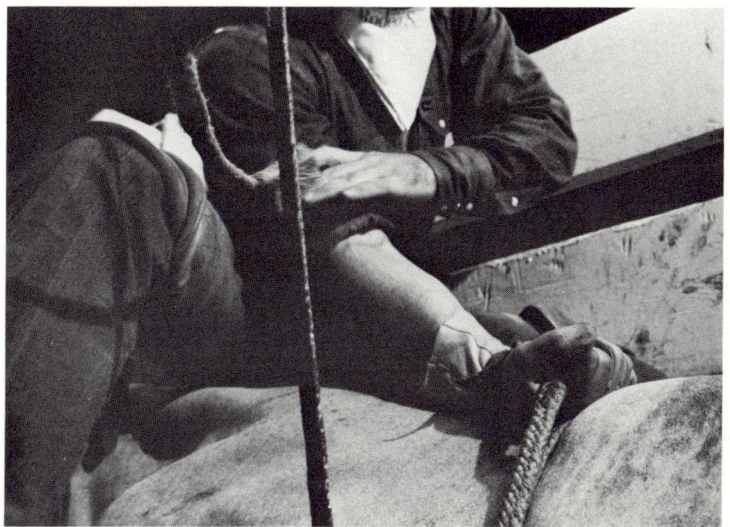

Top: Bull rider firmly grips plaited bull rope, ready to ride

Bottom: Seated on his mount, the bull rider waits to give the signal for the gate to be swung open and the ride to begin

These bulls may look docile, but they are pure dynamite when they leave the bucking chute

A champion bull rider on a champion bull during a winning ride

The eight-second ride is over. An exuberant cowboy throws his hat in the air, acknowledges the audience's applause, and signals his winning ride with upraised forefingers

Bull rider heading for a "wreck." Sometimes referred to as "going into orbit"

A fallen bullfighting clown after being "freight trained" by a cranky bull

"Sitting up fine," during the good ride

Rider in trouble

Bull rider losing his seat

There is no graceful way to dismount from a bucking bull

Clowns in dressing room before the rodeo

Rodeo clowns may look funny to the audience, and indeed some of them are strictly comedians. They perform between the events, entertaining the audience while the chutes are being loaded. To the bull rider in trouble the bullfighting clown is anything but funny. He is literally a lifesaver. The face paint, baggy pants, and fright wigs cannot fully hide their incredible athletic ability. It is their speed, agility, and courage in distracting an enraged bull that can save a fallen bull rider from disaster. ★

Bullfighting clowns relaxing between events

Bullfighting clown uses a foam rubber lined barrel as a barrier between himself and the bull. A favorite gag is for another clown inside the barrel to wave a white flag of surrender. A sure crowd-pleaser

Fallen bullfighter scrambles to evade bull

Sometimes it makes the most sense to run for it

It's over. Cowboys and cowgirls leave for home, or the next rodeo. Some cowboys travel over eighty thousand miles a year. They call it "going down the road." ★

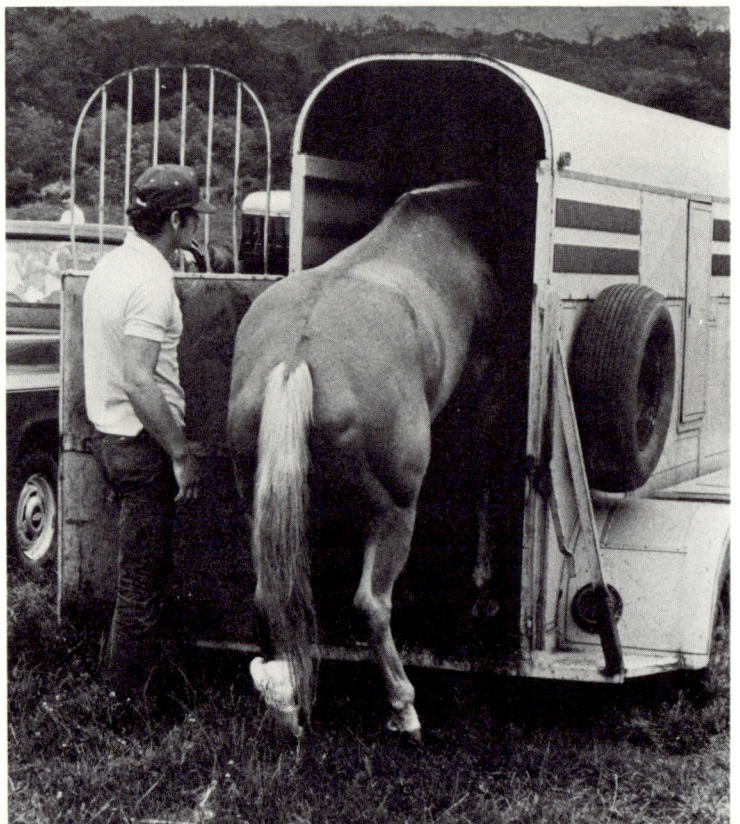

MURRAY TINKELMAN,
artist, photographer, teacher, lecturer, and honorary cowboy, was born in Brooklyn, New York. He studied art at the Cooper Union School of Art and at The Brooklyn Museum Art School. He has received over 150 major professional awards, over seventy of them from the Society of Illustrators, and his work is represented in the permanent collections of the Brooklyn Museum and the Smithsonian Institution among many others.

He is Associate Professor in the Department of Visual Communications, College of Visual and Performing Arts at Syracuse University, New York.

Mr. Tinkelman lives in Peekskill, New York, with his wife and two daughters.

j791
Tinkelman, Murray

Rodeo